Nutrition

Vitamins Are Vital

Kristin Petrie

ABDO
Publishing Company

visit us at
www.abdopub.com

Printed in the United States.

Cover Photo: Corbis
Interior Photos: Corbis pp. 1, 5, 7, 9, 11, 13, 14, 15, 16-17, 19, 20, 23, 24, 25, 27, 29

Editors: Kate A. Conley, Stephanie Hedlund, Kristianne E. Vieregger
Art Direction: Neil Klinepier

Library of Congress Cataloging-in-Publication Data

Petrie, Kristin, 1970-
    Vitamins are vital / Kristin Petrie.
        p. cm. -- (Nutrition)
    Summary: Describes different kinds of vitamins and minerals, what foods provide these nutrients, and how they are used by the body.
    ISBN 1-59197-406-2
    1. Vitamins in human nutrition--Juvenile literature. [1. Vitamins. 2. Nutrition.] I. Title.

QP771.P48 2003
613.2'86--dc21

2002043626

Contents

Vitamins & Minerals 4

Vitamins 6

The B Vitamins 8

Vitamin C 10

Vitamin A 12

Vitamin D 14

Vitamin E 16

Vitamin K 18

Minerals 20

Calcium 22

Iron 24

Water 26

Supplements 28

Glossary 30

Saying It 31

Web Sites 31

Index 32

Vitamins & Minerals

You've probably heard that vitamins and minerals are important. In fact, *vita* means "life" in Latin. Though vitamins and minerals are vital for our health, our bodies cannot make most of them. So, we need to eat a variety of foods that provide our bodies with different vitamins and minerals.

Vitamins and minerals are **micronutrients**. However, they do not give you energy or calories. So, why do you need them? Without vitamins and minerals, thousands of **reactions** in your body could not take place.

Vitamins and minerals help with reactions such as obtaining energy from food, producing red blood cells, helping your bones grow, and keeping your skin healthy. The reactions happen when vitamins and minerals connect with other **nutrients** like pieces of a puzzle.

What Are Vitamins & Minerals?

Vitamins and minerals are necessary for life. But, what are they exactly? Vitamins are organic molecules found in food. Minerals are inorganic molecules found in food. Your body needs small amounts of vitamins and minerals to stay healthy!

One of the **nutrients** that vitamins and minerals connect with is water. Your body needs water every day to stay healthy. Continue reading to learn what vitamins, minerals, and water do for your body.

Vitamins and minerals can be found in many different foods. That is why it is good to eat a large variety every day.

Vitamins

There are two kinds of vitamins—those that love water and those that love fat! Vitamins that love water are called **water soluble**. Vitamins that love fat are called **fat soluble**.

Vitamins B and C make up the group of water soluble vitamins. They are found in many foods, and they often work together in the body. Being water soluble means these vitamins can move freely in your bloodstream. They are also absorbed into your cells fairly easily.

Your body does not store water soluble vitamins. So, after your cells have taken what they need, anything left over is released in your urine. For this reason, you need to eat foods containing vitamins B and C often.

Vitamins A, D, E, and K make up the fat soluble group of vitamins. They need fat from your diet to be absorbed and transported in your body. You receive fat soluble vitamins from the fatty and oily parts of foods.

Unlike their water-loving friends, **fat soluble** vitamins can be stored in body fat and the liver. Storing too many fat soluble vitamins in your body can be toxic. It is rare, however, for a person to get too many fat soluble vitamins from food. This usually happens when people take too many vitamin **supplements**.

Fresh vegetables are filled with vitamins.

The B Vitamins

The B vitamins are actually a group of eight **water soluble** vitamins. They are important to many of your body's functions. One of their most important jobs is releasing energy from the carbohydrates, fats, and proteins that you have eaten.

The B vitamins have many other jobs, too. For example, the B vitamins keep your skin healthy and help your body fight germs and infections. They also help you think, make decisions, and move all your body parts.

The B Vitamins

thiamine (B_1)

riboflavin (B_2)

niacin

pyridoxine (B_6)

folic acid

cobalamin (B_{12})

biotin

pantothenic acid

Where Can You Find the B Vitamins?

Great sources of the B vitamins are whole grain or enriched breads and cereals, dried beans, milk, eggs, nuts, and green leafy vegetables such as spinach and broccoli. Meats such as beef, chicken, and fish also contain different B vitamins.

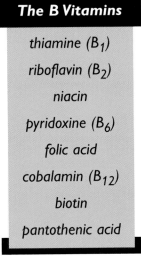

B vitamins are found in a wide variety of foods, so it is easy to make sure you are getting enough.

Vitamin C

Orange juice, anyone? You know that oranges and orange juice are good for you. You also know that they are high in vitamin C. But, what exactly does vitamin C do?

This **water soluble** vitamin has many jobs. Like the B vitamins, it sometimes acts as a helper. As a helper, vitamin C is involved in **reactions** that cause the protein collagen to form. Your bones, skin, and even your arteries are made of collagen.

Vitamin C also acts as an **antioxidant**. It helps fight off germs and infections. If you give your body a daily dose of foods rich in vitamin C, you will have a stronger defense against colds, viruses, and all kinds of illnesses.

Where Can You Find Vitamin C?

Oranges and orange juice are not the only places to find vitamin C. Fruits such as honeydew, watermelon, strawberries, raspberries, lemons, and kiwi have lots of it. Many vegetables such as bell peppers, tomatoes, potatoes, and broccoli are also good sources.

Opposite page: Vitamin C helps prevent your skin from easily bruising. Luckily, it is found in many tasty foods.

Vitamin A

Have you ever wondered how you are able to see? Vitamin A's biggest role is to help your vision. The pigments in your eyes need this **fat soluble** vitamin to see colors and to see at night.

Did you know that vitamin A also has other roles? It is important in reproduction, healthy skin, immunity, and the making of red blood cells. Without enough vitamin A, the body may suffer in many ways, from dry skin to night blindness.

Where Can You Find Vitamin A?

Vitamin A is found in a wide variety of foods. The most well known, of course, is the carrot. Other great sources are apricots, nectarines, and cantaloupe. Vegetables with vitamin A include spinach, pumpkins, and sweet potatoes.

Opposite page: Eating carrots, which are filled with vitamin A, will help you read your favorite books.

Vitamin D

Which vitamin can we thank for strong bones and bright, white teeth? Vitamin D, of course! This **fat soluble** vitamin helps your body absorb the mineral calcium, which forms and maintains strong bones. Children who do not receive enough vitamin D have weak, slow-growing bones that may not be straight. Vitamin D may also help prevent some kinds of **cancer**.

Milk is a good source of vitamin D.

Where Can You Find Vitamin D?

Milk, fortified with vitamin D, is the fastest and easiest way to receive the amount of vitamin D that your body needs. Other sources include eggs, butter, tuna, and salmon. Your amazing body can also make vitamin D when you are in the sun!

To make vitamin D, your body needs about 20 to 30 minutes of sun on your hands and face two to three times per week. Be sure to drink plenty of milk, especially in the winter, when you may not be outside as much.

Vitamin E

The next time you're walking on a balance beam, thank vitamin E! This **fat soluble** vitamin keeps the **nerves** in your muscles working well. It allows you to walk straight, move your eyeballs, and bend and point your fingers.

Vitamin E can do more than just keep your nerves tuned. Vitamin E is also an **antioxidant**. And, the next time you take a deep breath, vitamin E can help. That's because it protects your lungs from pollution.

Where Can You Find Vitamin E?

We receive most of our vitamin E from the vegetable oils that our foods are made with. Other sources include sunflower seeds, peanuts, spinach, and milk.

Thanks to vitamin E, this girl can turn the pages of her book.

Vitamin K

You would really be hurting without vitamin K. Why? Every time you scrape your knee or cut your finger, vitamin K comes to the rescue. This **fat soluble** vitamin helps your blood clot. Clotting slows the bleeding and keeps germs out. Vitamin K is so important that you probably got a shot of it right after you were born so your little body had the clotting power it needed.

Where Can You Find Vitamin K?

Green, leafy vegetables are the best sources of vitamin K. They include broccoli, spinach, and dark lettuce such as romaine. Vitamin K can also be found in foods such as milk, cheese, yogurt, meats, eggs, cereals, and fruits.

Opposite page: Vitamin K can be made within your body. But, it is best to eat some leafy veggies to make sure you are getting enough.

Minerals

You know vitamins are important for staying healthy. But, don't forget about minerals! They are equally important for good health. Potassium and sodium, for example, allow your eyes to blink and your legs to bend. These minerals transmit **nerve** impulses—without them, you'd be like a wet noodle.

You've probably learned about minerals in your science classes. Yes, minerals are tiny pieces of rocks and metals. Luckily, we don't have to eat rocks and pieces of metal to get our minerals. The foods you eat have minerals in them.

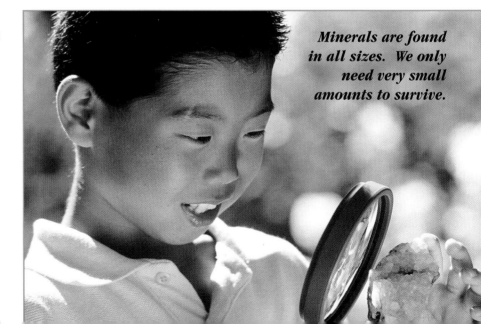

Minerals are found in all sizes. We only need very small amounts to survive.

Scientists have divided minerals into two groups. They are called macrominerals and microminerals. Microminerals are also called trace minerals.

The word *macro* means "large." Don't be fooled by the name, however. Macrominerals are tiny. We call them macro because we need them in larger amounts than we need the trace minerals. An important macromineral is calcium.

The word *micro* means "very small." The microminerals are named this because we need them in very small amounts. Iron is an important micromineral.

Minerals in Food

How did your foods get minerals? There are lots of ways! For example, carrots and potatoes received minerals from the soil they grew in. Hamburgers and steaks got their minerals from the grass the cows ate. And, fish received minerals from the water they swam in.

The Minerals

The macrominerals are calcium, phosphorous, magnesium, sodium, potassium, chloride, and sulfur. The trace minerals include iron, manganese, copper, iodine, zinc, cobalt, fluoride, and selenium.

Calcium

If you are between 11 and 18 years old, your body is using this macromineral like a race car uses gas! You can almost see your legs getting longer! This is due to the work of vitamin D, calcium, and other minerals.

Getting enough calcium is very important. You want your bones to be as strong as possible. Stocking up on calcium now will help you avoid problems such as **osteoporosis**.

Where Can You Find Calcium?

Milk is the most obvious and easiest way to get your calcium. But, don't forget that yogurt, cheese, frozen yogurt, and milk shakes work, too. Green, leafy vegetables, many breakfast cereals, and juices that have been fortified with calcium are also great sources.

Opposite page: Your body has more calcium than any other mineral, and 99 percent of it is found in your bones.

Iron

Iron is the body's gold. This micromineral is so important that it is found in every cell of your body. Iron helps in **reactions** that make new cells, hormones, and **nerve** transmitters. Its most important job, however, is to move oxygen from your lungs to every other part of your body.

Many people do not get enough iron. So, it's a good idea to make an effort to eat some foods rich in iron regularly. Look for breakfast cereals **fortified** with iron. In addition, drink some orange juice or eat an orange along with your breakfast cereal. Why? Vitamin C helps you absorb even more iron from foods.

Where Can You Find Iron?

Good sources of iron include red meats, dried beans, baked potatoes with the skin, apricots, and raisins. You can also find iron in many fortified cereals and health drinks.

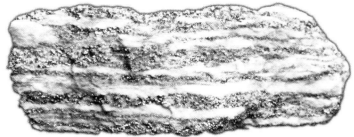

This rock has iron and other minerals in it, but thankfully you don't have to eat it to stay healthy!

Your parents will be able to help make sure that you are eating enough vitamins and minerals.

Water

Vitamins and minerals often work with the **nutrient** water. You cannot live without water. It makes up more than half of your body weight! It is the main component in your blood and your cells. It also makes up your saliva, sweat, and tears.

Water is needed for all of your body's functions. It helps break down the food you eat, produces energy from nutrients, and gets rid of the leftovers in your urine. Without enough water, your body will become **dehydrated**, and you won't feel or function well.

You receive water from the tap or in bottles. Water also comes from drinks such as milk and juice. It is in the food you eat, too. However, to replace the water that is lost, you should drink a few glasses of it each day.

Water is often called the forgotten nutrient. However, many people argue that it is the most important.

Supplements

Now you know how vitamins, minerals, and water are important to your growing body. With all these important jobs, it may seem impossible to get enough. Actually, it's easy to get all the vitamins and minerals from the foods you eat. You just need to take a little time to make good food choices.

It may seem simpler to just take vitamins and minerals in a pill form. Studies have shown, however, that people who eat a variety of foods are healthier than those who eat a poor diet and take vitamin and mineral pills.

More importantly, health benefits may not come from the actual vitamins and minerals but from how they work together! For example, eating berries of all sorts seems to protect people from certain types of **cancer**. However, taking many pills with the same vitamins found in berries does not always have the same result.

Here is another way to think of it. If you sing or play an instrument, you may not sound that great on your own. But, put your voice or instrument with a bunch of others, and it sounds pretty good! This may be how foods benefit our health. All alone, vitamins and minerals are not impressive. But mix them up with the other **nutrients** found in food, and you'll get some great results.

To give your body benefits such as healthy skin, good vision, and protection against diseases, eat a wide variety of foods. Vitamins and minerals are an important part of your diet. So, eat right and stay healthy!

Many people take a daily supplement even though it is not necessary if you eat a balanced, healthy diet.

Glossary

antioxidant - a substance that protects cells from damage.

cancer - any of a group of often deadly diseases characterized by an abnormal growth of cells that destroys healthy tissues and organs.

dehydrated - the result of too little water. A person becomes dehydrated when the fluid used and lost is not replaced.

fat soluble - able to dissolve and move freely in fat.

fortified - having one or more nutrients not normally found in a food added to increase that food's nutritional value.

micronutrients - the smallest nutrients found in food. They include vitamins and minerals.

nerves - clusters of cells that the body uses to send messages to and from the brain.

nutrient - a substance found in food and used in the body to promote growth, maintenance, and repair.

osteoporosis - a disease where the bones lose calcium, causing them to become weak.

reaction - the combination of two or more substances that produces something new, such as energy.

supplements - a source of nutrients taken in addition to food.

water soluble - able to dissolve and move freely in water.

Saying It

antioxidant - an-tee-AHK-suh-duhnt
carbohydrate - kahr-boh-HI-drayt
collagen - KAH-luh-juhn
dehydrate - dee-HI-drayt
immunity - ih-MYOO-nuh-tee

osteoporosis - ahs-tee-oh-puh-ROH-suhs
pigment - PIG-muhnt
soluble - SAHL-yuh-buhl
toxic - TAHK-sihk

Web Sites

To learn more about vitamins and minerals, visit ABDO Publishing Company on the World Wide Web at **www.abdopub.com**. Web sites about nutrition are featured on our Book Links page. These links are routinely monitored and updated to provide the most current information available.

Index

A
antioxidants 10, 16

B
B vitamins 6, 8, 10

C
calcium 14, 21, 22
calories 4
cancer 14, 28
carbohydrates 8
collagen 10

F
fat 6, 8
fat soluble 6, 7, 12, 14, 16,
    18
foods 4, 6, 7, 10, 20, 24,
    26, 28, 29

I
iron 21, 24

M
macrominerals 21, 22
microminerals 21, 24
micronutrients 4

N
nutrients 4, 5, 26, 29

O
organs 7, 12, 16, 20, 24
osteoporosis 22

P
potassium 20
protein 8, 10

S
sodium 20
supplements 7, 28

V
vitamin A 6, 12
vitamin C 6, 10, 24
vitamin D 6, 14, 22
vitamin E 6, 16
vitamin K 6, 18

W
water 5, 6, 7, 26, 28
water soluble 6, 8, 10